P9-DXF-895

THE SNOOPY COLLECTION

THE SNOOPY COLLECTION

EDITED AND DESIGNED BY J-C SUARES

INTRODUCTION BY NANCY SMART

PHOTOGRAPHS BY DON HAMERMAN

A World Almanac Publication

Stewart, Tabori & Chang, Publishers, Inc.

New York, New York

First published in 1982.

Paperback edition distributed in the United States
by Ballantine Books, a division of Random House,
Inc., and in Canada by Random House of Canada, Ltd.

Hardcover edition published by Stewart, Tabori and Chang, Inc.

Library of Congress Catalog Card Number (paperback edition): 81-71774
Newspaper Enterprise Association ISBN 0-911818-30-8
Ballantine Books ISBN 0-345-30340-7
Stewart, Tabori & Chang ISBN 0-941434-15-X

Newspaper Enterprise Association, Inc.
World Almanac Publications
Jane D. Flatt, Publisher
200 Park Avenue
New York, New York 10166

Front cover photograph courtesy of Familiar, Ltd., Kobe, Japan
Back cover photograph by Don Hamerman

FOREWORD

by J-C Suares

I have a fabulous winter coat that cost me a small fortune. It is a dark blue coat manufactured in Canada with a magnificent black mink collar. It is definitely one of my favorite possessions and I'll wear it till it falls apart.

But my very favorite possession, the one I'll have long after the coat has turned to shreds, is a little SNOOPY pin I bought in the Denver Airport a few years ago. I wear it all the time, and its value cannot be estimated because it brings me good luck. I wear it with all my outfits, even the great coat, and for every important event. I wore it at my wedding, on long transatlantic flights, at business lunches. I even wore it on television.

Wearing that SNOOPY pin makes me feel like I'm always with a friend, the friend I met through the years and years of reading PEANUTS®. I know him and I like him. I also think that he understands me. And I'm not alone. Millions of people feel the same way and keep plush SNOOPY® dolls and innumerable other objects bearing his name and his likeness in their homes. This book is about those fabulous objects.

The idea for this book came about one day when I stumbled into a showroom in the Pan Am building in New York that was devoted entirely to PEANUTS products. There were a thousand different things displayed in it, from games to calendars, from cups to pianos. It looked like a future exhibit in the Smithsonian. So I thought, if the Frick Collection deserves a house and the Armand Hammer Collection deserves a house, then why not this one? It tells as much or more about our times and our heroes than any other!

Therefore, I decided to compile a book about that SNOOPY Collection, an art book, mind you. And I would pick the most interesting and beautiful items at my disposal and commission a great photographer to take pictures of them much the same way he would document the possessions of a museum. Here it is, and I want Snoopy himself to know that I would not have done a more lavish job for Rodin himself.

On Saturday nights, Spike, Snoopy's forerunner, would promptly remind Schulz's father when it was time to pick up the Sunday papers.

INTRODUCTION

by Nancy Smart

1. ROOTS

When Snoopy first appeared on America's comic strip pages, his floppy ears and innocent face typified cuddly, trusting puppyhood. This year, at thirty-two, Snoopy is still lovable in his myriad roles and guises, but he has become a good deal more than an innocent puppy to his millions of fans.

Snoopy began to grow in the imagination of PEANUTS® creator, Charles Schulz, long before the first PEANUTS® strip appeared. Snoopy had two real-life forerunners — Schulz family pets — although neither was a beagle. Snooky, a Boston Bull, was given to the two-year-old Schulz to be a companion for the only child. Schulz vividly recalls the pain when, ten years later, his father had to tell him that Snooky had been killed by a car. The death strengthened Schulz's attachment to Snooky and provided a recurring theme of the PEANUTS® strip: the affection between a boy and his dog.

When he was thirteen, Schulz got his second dog. He remembers: "Spike wasn't a pure pointer. He was heavier and not as big, but he was just wild, almost uncontrollable, and he was bright, extremely bright." Just how wild was Spike? Wild enough to make "Ripley's Believe It or Not" on February 22, 1937. This was Schulz's first published drawing, made when he was fifteen. Spike's sketch is captioned: "A hunting dog that eats pins, tacks and razor blades is owned by C. F. Schulz, St. Paul, Minnesota."

Spike was as imaginative as he was tough. His varied diet included rubber balls and spaghetti as well as sharp objects and he comprehended fifty words, but Spike's hobbies were most notable. Every Saturday night at nine, Spike would remind Schulz's father that it was time to take their weekly drive to fetch the newspapers. Spike's antics during their years together provided Schulz with a wealth of material that would later surface in the world of Snoopy.

When Charles Schulz conceived his comic strip, he intended to make one of the characters a dog named Sniffy. But Schulz, an avid reader and student of the popular cartoonists of the time, soon discovered that a comic magazine already featured a dog named Sniffy. He knew he had to change Sniffy's name, but to what? Then he remembered his mother's choice for a name if the family acquired another dog. Not long after, in October, 1950, Snoopy, the lop-eared beagle, was officially born as PEANUTS® made its debut in nine U.S. newspapers. Years later, Schulz would learn that "Snoopy" had been considered — but, luckily, rejected — as a name for one of Walt Disney's seven dwarfs.

Schulz recalls: "Snoopy grew out of the way people talk to their dogs. People who become very close to their pets, if you observe them, say things to their pets and then respond as they think their pet would respond. This is really what happened with Snoopy."

The cartoonist never intended to have Snoopy talk. But the idea that this dog might be able to *think* grew naturally out of Snoopy's developing personality. "Snoopy was always slightly independent and precocious. That's what made him different."

From the very beginning, Snoopy was smart. As Schulz watched neighborhood kids playing with their pets, he was fascinated by how tolerant the dogs were of their young masters' silliness, and how cleverly they responded to the children's demands. He remembered things Spike had done, like fetching potatoes from the basement on request. Intelligence — indeed, wisdom — independence, precociousness, and a certain vulnerability were to be Snoopy's main traits. Although Schulz didn't fully realize it immediately, these qualities would allow Snoopy to develop limitless appeal in the comic strip, on film and TV screens, and on thousands of items of merchandise.

Snoopy represents a unique character development in cartoon history. No dog, appearing as a companion to human characters, had ever before displayed a complex personality. Yet Snoopy, underneath his playful exterior, was already as smart as his young master.

But puppies, like people, need time to grow. The very early Snoopy looked a little like a baby doll with round head and ears, a nicely proportioned, puppy-like body, and delicately pointed paws. His thought balloons had to get his ideas across without benefit of words. In the early years, he had only four expressions: "arf, arf"; "gulp"; "♡♡"; and "!!!"

1952

Soon, Snoopy's concepts and the words he used to express them began to increase rapidly. In *PEANUTS Jubilee*, published in 1975, Schulz remarked on Snoopy's growing ability to "think": "This is when the strip turned its first important corner. Snoopy became slightly superior to the kids in the strip. Most of the time he won out over them."

Snoopy can almost always outscore Lucy when she's crabby, and can steal Linus's blanket at will, but when Sally accuses him of leading a useless life, he cranes his neck down from his doghouse and gives her a big wet kiss on her nose. "Just the thing for turning aside anger," he remarks. Clearly this superior dog has a very "human" affection for his companions.

Although Snoopy's personality developed rapidly, it became increasingly apparent to Schulz that his physical characteristics were not keeping up. It was several years after Snoopy's creation before Schulz found the perfect visual image to match Snoopy's complex intellect. In retrospect, Schulz sees this as a natural growth process: "There was a period where I think he was drawn terribly. As I look back upon it, I can't believe the way I was drawing him, but this happens all the time. You draw from day to day, and you have no comprehension that your style is changing and you're drawing characters in a certain way. The characters get fatter, they get thinner, larger, and smaller, but in the case of Snoopy, he became terribly distorted and I had no idea until I saw the reprint books a year or two later. Then you have to try to bring your style back."

Strips from 1958 show Schulz working on, and finally mastering, the art of drawing Snoopy. Not surprisingly, Snoopy looks less like a real dog than before. His nose has grown longer, his ears narrower, and his front feet are broader. He still looks trusting and cheerful, but older, more experienced — he's nobody's fool. Snoopy finally is ready to show his stuff; two remaining changes would fully unlock his potential.

The first of these changes was getting up on his hind legs to walk on two feet. Snoopy had already grown larger, but from now on, he'd also be taller, capable of more kinds of physical movement, on equal footing with the kids.

"Letting Snoopy think and walk around on his hind legs also made him superior to the kids in the strip, since he could go his own way and exhibit an imagination that was unmatched by the rest of the characters," explains Schulz. "It was difficult to keep him from becoming the real hero of the strip."

The second change was that Snoopy stopped going *into* the dog house and started going *on top of* it. This throne-like perspective not only opened up new possibilities for action, but also established Snoopy's position in the strip as the lofty dreamer, the philosopher, and the confident, cheerful explorer looking for new worlds to conquer.

At heart, though, our intellectual super-dog remains a realist, only slightly put off by having to climb down from his perch to check out the dinner bowl. The first time he falls off his doghouse, he admits that "Life is full of rude awakenings." It's this blending of Snoopy's limitless abilities in the world of his imagination with his all-too-human imperfections in real life that endears him to his fans. These same qualities explain in part the seemingly limitless appetite of those fans to surround themselves with images and representations of Snoopy, a small sampling of which are included in this book.

1959

3. MODERN
TIMES

It's possible that most of PEANUTS'® readers empathize with Charlie Brown, but most of us would rather *be* Snoopy. Like Charlie Brown, our daydreams are usually unexceptional fantasies firmly based in our everyday realities. Only Charlie Brown would admit to such dull fantasies as impressing the little red-haired girl and getting everyone to like him. But Snoopy's fantasies are anything but mundane. The number and quality of his daydreams set him apart from us, as surely as they tempt us to believe and dream along with him. His rich fantasy life involves us; his reckless willingness to plunge headlong into adventure is contagious. Never mind that Snoopy's visions occasionally end by crashing him headlong into the wall of reality. No matter what the outcome, he keeps believing he's the best, and by believing, often achieves it.

By the late '50s and early '60s, Snoopy's fantasy world began to expand. Like stars coming out on a summer night, Snoopy's daydreams would pop out full strength after the merest twinkle of an idea. First, with his dance routine. He's the happy hoofer, even if no one else can hear the music, but he's glad to find a partner, be it only a falling leaf with big-band rhythm. Turn the page to another day, another week, and Snoopy's a hot-dogging surfer, a sophisticated gourmet, a secret agent. He might blow Linus over into a swimming pool pretending to be the Big Bad Wolf. Or soar through the skies as a bald eagle, until he falls painfully short of his target, never having taken "swoop" lessons. He's made an art out of sleeping. He knows what a broken heart is. He'll befriend a snowman and cry to see it melt. His ears can become the antennae of a short-wave radio or the blades of a helicopter.

The one thing Snoopy can't seem to be is shy. In fact, during his first flights of fancy, Snoopy almost ran away with the strip.

"Snoopy has almost no restrictions," says Schulz. "He can go in any direction. He kind of breaks the boundaries of sex and race and everything, really. You can get away with things coming from Snoopy that wouldn't be quite as funny if they were coming from one of the kids."

For the cartoonist, controlling Snoopy can be a struggle: "For a while, Snoopy was starting to dominate the strip and I didn't want that to happen. So I always come back to the kids in the strip rather than him. I could draw Snoopy every day. He could easily carry a strip by himself because he's the easiest one to draw and he's the easiest one to think up ideas for, but I think it would be a big mistake. The strip is not just about Snoopy. It's about all of them."

Schulz and Snoopy at home. Even top dogs need love and affection.

In 1965, despite Schulz's efforts, Snoopy seemed to take control anyway. Snoopy, the World War I Flying Ace, was about to become the world's most popular pilot. His creator discovered he had more than he'd bargained for when he got the idea for this dogged war hero: "Next to Linus's blanket, it was the best single idea I ever thought of. As soon as I thought of it, I knew I had something really good. It was supposed to be a parody of World War I movies, but it didn't work out that way. I drew the one Sunday page, and I knew I had something. Then I drew some more. I kept drawing them, and it just worked."

Ten years after the Flying Ace first appeared, NASA named the Apollo 10 landing module (LEM) "Snoopy," and he was honored from outer space when astronaut John Young transmitted Snoopy's picture back to earth from 110,000 miles away. Snoopy had orbited the moon and literally skyrocketed to greater fame.

The Red Baron/World War I Flying Ace sequence was only the first of Snoopy's longer-running fantasies. He's also well-known as the Great American Novelist, big man on campus Joe Cool, and the Wimbledon Tennis Champ, to name just a few. He plays all these roles to entertain himself — and us. When his adventures leave him "bottoms-up" in his water dish, or suspended face down from a tree branch, he automatically heads for sanctuary, the roof of his doghouse, to think things over, and invariably begins to plan a new flight into fancy.

4. LICENSING OF SNOOPY

Snoopy can travel the world — and out of it — and be anything he wants to be in his fantasies. Simultaneously he travels the real world in many forms as the result of an unusual character licensing program. In the last 20 years, no other character has come close to challenging "Snoopy" as the single most successful and most desired name.

In 1981, the more than 100 companies licensed by United Feature Syndicate to use Snoopy's name and those of the other PEANUTS® characters sold at the retail level several hundred million dollars of merchandise. (Both UFS and Schulz's Creative Associates are privately held companies and do not release financial information.)

Here are some of the facts behind the world-wide phenomenon:

● Adults use SNOOPY products a lot more than children. For example, of the 5,000 PEANUTS products on the market today, less than 15 to 20 percent are toys.

● SNOOPY books have been translated into twenty-two languages and have sold more than 100,000,000 copies during the past thirty years.

● There are at least 30,000 U.S. retail outlets for SNOOPY products, ranging from Bloomingdale's to local bowling alleys.

● A plush SNOOPY® doll resides in the permanent collection of the Smithsonian Institution.

● There are 300 "best selling" items, which include SNOOPY T-shirts (all sizes and both genders), books and calendar/date books, plush dolls and doll wardrobe kits, and greeting cards.

- "Snoopy" has become a brand name.
- Ninety percent of the PEANUTS merchandise sold is SNOOPY products.
- Quality control is maintained through a strictly enforced approvals system operated by Creative Associates and United Feature Syndicate. Even the biggest and most successful licensees have had to remove items from the marketplace when they have not met standards set by the two companies.
- There are approximately 100 professional designers who are employed full time by licensees to develop new products and new designs for existing products.
- Being a licensee can be extremely lucrative regardless of the size of the company involved. J.P. Stevens, Inc., a giant in the textile business, sold $7,000,000 worth of SNOOPY linens the first year they were on the market. Aviva Enterprises (jewelry, trophies, luggage) was started with a $5,000 investment in 1968 and had sales of nearly $3,000,000 annually by 1971.

Snoopy's sister Belle modeling part of her extensive wardrobe. Here, Baby Doll Pajamas.

The first licensing of PEANUTS was to the publishing firm of Rinehart & Co., Inc. (now Holt, Rinehart & Winston) which began publishing reprints of the strip in 1952, just two years after its inception. The books sold well from the beginning — and still do thirty years later. But the first indication that there was a huge desire for new, specially created products came with the publication of *Happiness Is a Warm Puppy*, which was original Schulz art, not reprints of the strip. The slim volume, published by Determined Productions of San Francisco, was the book sensation of 1962-63, shooting to the top of the bestseller lists and ultimately selling more than 1,500,000 copies. Today Determined Productions is the largest PEANUTS licensee.

Schulz and his colleagues learned an important lesson with the success of that first book. It is better to have the appeal of Snoopy and the other characters "pull" products into the market than to try to "push" them into the market and create boredom and overexposure. The cartoonist feels the licensing has worked out to be "almost flawless in its concept," because "we were selective."

"It would have been very easy for me to turn the whole thing over to a licensing company or just let the syndicate do whatever it wanted, but I remained involved in everything that was done. I watched over the development of each product. In better than 90 percent of the cases, people with ideas approached me first.

"We try to do each product as well as we can. We've always held down the number of products; we've never let the licensing run wild. Even today we could be doing much more than we are doing. If anyone looks and says 'Boy, they sure have done a lot of things,' he should realize that we could have done a lot more and maybe spoiled it, but we handled it all very carefully, step-by-step and, I feel, always tried to do the best we could."

We don't know whether Snoopy would agree with that judgment, but millions of his fans who number among their favorite possessions at least one souvenir, replica or memento of the lop-eared beagle probably would agree with the sentiment expressed by Joe Garagiola in his introduction to the book *Sandlot PEANUTS*: "They say everybody in America has two dogs — their own and Snoopy."

Right: Snoopy in the annual Macy's Thanksgiving Day Parade. Once he was even launched as a Goodyear blimp. (Photo: Bruno Zehnder)

GIANT SNOOPY

As huggable as they are lovable, plush dolls invite everyone to play. The plush fabric is woven (rather than knitted) from the softest yarns, and then tufted like a deep pile rug. The result: the cuddliest, fluffiest, most durable stuffed dolls on the market today.

Below: Snoopy and his brother Spike are five feet tall and full of fun. Sister Belle is slightly smaller and definitely more demure. Clothing shown is custom-made. *Right:* Snoopy in black tie.

Four plush SNOOPY®
dolls rise to the occasion.
Clockwise from top left:
Flying Ace, Santa, Red
Nightshirt, Warm-up
Suit.

The plush SNOOPY®
dolls come in sizes for
everybody, but the most
popular models are the
Baby and Medium
SNOOPY dolls.

Just cruising along: a
crew of plush SNOOPY®
dolls.

SNOOPY'S WARDROBE

For today's well-dressed beagle, feeling good means looking good. Thanks to the talents of Snoopy's international staff of professional clothing designers, Snoopy is well prepared to dress up for almost any occasion.

Below: A small sampling from Snoopy's eclectic wardrobe collection. *Right:* Looking especially cuddly in his striped sleeper outfit, Snoopy gears up for bedtime stories.

Doing the SNOOPY
strut in the official signa-
ture denim jeans.

SNOOPY

His score is love — but
he wins every game.

Trumpets sound when Sir Snoopy arrives.

School bag of jersey-backed vinyl with back-pack straps and SNOOPY art on front flap.

Astronaut Snoopy in
shiny silver space suit.

The intricate styling of the Scottish costume inspires Snoopy to do a real Highland Fling.

Coordinated tank top and shorts add color to Snoopy's fitness routine.

Like all the other wardrobe items, a dapper Sherlock Holmes outfit comes in sizes to fit both the Baby and Medium plush SNOOPY® dolls.

Folding deck chair promises adventurous dreams of sun, surf, and sand.

BABY SNOOPY

Below: Tiny baby booties made of the softest woven cotton help muffle the pitter-patter of active puppy paws.
Right: Baby Snoopy in diapers sits on a Snoopy blanket.

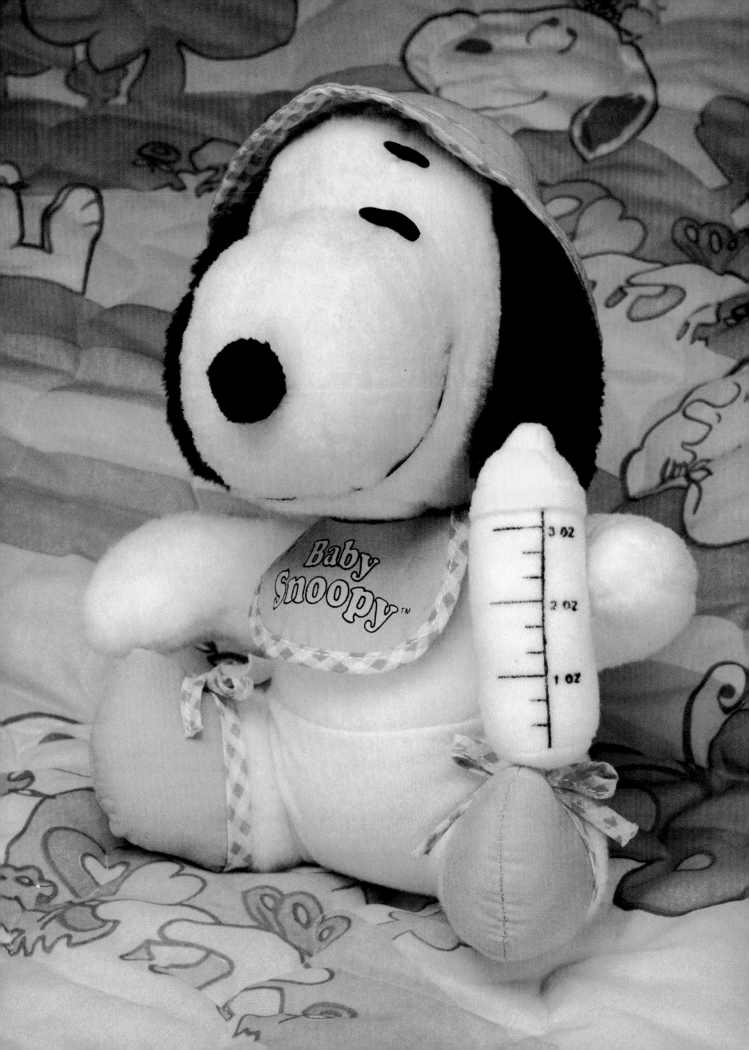

SNOOPY IN MOTION

It's virtually impossible for Snoopy to stand still in the face of adventure, and most of the time, we'd like to go with him. These toys all capture some aspect of Snoopy's fantasy life and are either friction-powered (no batteries needed) or hand-manipulated to change course or position.

Below: Vinyl Tub-Time SNOOPY is a clean machine because he's completely washable and fully jointed. Comes with his own bathrobe, bath brush and mono-grammed towel.

Right: The world's greatest boxer packs a powerful punch while Woodstock watches and wobbles from atop the springform punching bag.

Over easy or scrambled, eggs really flip when the world's greatest cook is in charge. Plastic SNOOPY has windup action and all the finesse of a master chef.

Snoopy may march to a
different drummer, but
here he strikes a snappy
beat.

The Flying Ace swoops up, down, and sideways in his SNOOPY Biplane Balance Toy for ages three and up. Works on the principle of two-way balance and motion. No motorized parts.

Snoopy may have picked up some of his athletic prowess from creator Charles Schulz who excels in hockey, tennis, and golf.

Snoopy has a special "swivel head" in the SNOOPY Doghouse Motorized Toy which requires gentle pressure on the rear wheels to make it go.

Vinyl Snoopy with plush
fabric ears and tail is
8½" high. Arms and legs
are movable.

SNOOPY PLATES

Charles Schulz's original art is used to
commemorate holidays and other special
occasions on fine porcelain plates. Each
edition is dated and production is limited
to the year of issue. Each plate measures
7½'' in diameter.

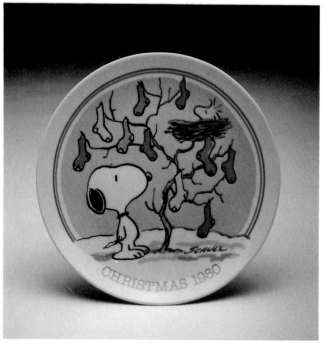

A selection of SNOOPY plates issued in recent years to commemorate Valentine's Day, Christmas, and Mother's Day. Plates issued in the early seventies are already considered valuable collector's items.

SNOOPY BEDDING

SNOOPY sheets, pillowcases, blankets and spreads can bring smiles to sleepy faces. Half the fun comes from picking out your own favorite patterns and colors from the many styles and sets available.

Kids love to run for cover under the soft warmth of a SNOOPY blanket.

Snoopy and Woodstock
star on pillows around
the world.

Bedmaking is made fun
with a SNOOPY
"Basketball" bedspread.

Standard size pillowcase
shows Snoopy in Beagle
Heaven—sound asleep.

Dogs are
born to
sleep in
the sun!

Home is where the heart is for Snoopy and Woodstock and any sleepy head. No-iron muslin pillowcase.

SNOOPY MUGS

When is a mug a SNOOPY mug? When it can make you laugh in the morning, get you cheerfully through the afternoon, keep your cocoa warm on a snowy evening, and is designed for celebrating all happy thoughts no matter what the time of day. All mugs are twelve ounces and made of white ceramic with colorful art and captions.

Right: SNOOPY mugs depict Snoopy weightlifting, kicking a football, and hitting a tennis ball. *Below*: Four parts of the United States are depicted: Florida, Chicago, Washington, D.C., and New Orleans.

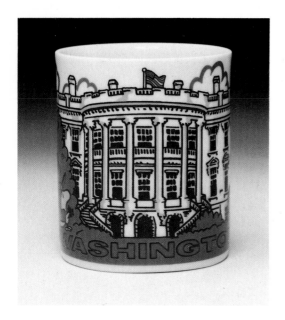

COLOR FORMS AND PUZZLES

Kids really get the picture when it comes to designing their own pictures featuring PEANUTS® characters. Colorforms Play Sets contain thirty-nine different plastic pieces, which stick like magic to the colorful workboard background surface. These sets are both fun and educational as they exercise six basic learning skills including finger dexterity, sense of color, and spatial awareness.

A scene from "Disco Snoopy" Colorforms Set. Workboard and plastic pieces never wear out and wipe clean with a damp cloth.

In this scene, Snoopy, his hockey stick, Woodstock, and Snoopy's dog dish are stick-on pieces.

SNOOPY jigsaw puzzle
contains 150 pieces and
measures 286 x 210 mm.
assembled.

CERAMICS

SNOOPY ceramics are designed to be used for kitchen, bath, living room, and tabletops anywhere. Each piece is carefully handpainted, and the entire collection is closely inspected to maintain the highest quality.

SNOOPY soap boxes
are white with color trim,
4¾"x 3¾".

From top-left down:
The Snoopy Bubble Tub can stash anything from bubble bath to bobby pins. 4½" high, 3" wide. Snoopy finds an oval soap dish a perfect place for good, clean fun. The quintessential Snoopy: his "Love" Heart Box. 2½" wide with lift-off lid.

You can count on a 6" ceramic "Joe Cool" Snoopy to know just where the action is.

Flower arranging is done by the book. SNOOPY vase is shown actual size.

Ah! Here it is! "A Beagle's Blooming Garden Guide"!

Plants and flowers
bloom in a SNOOPY
style that's hard not to
love. Actual size.

SNOOPY TELEPHONES

A variety of styles, shapes, and colors of SNOOPY telephones are manufactured all over the world. From whimsical play phones to witty real ones, Snoopy has made and received literally millions of calls. SNOOPY phones plug into regular household jacks, are made with both pushbutton and rotary dials, and are adjustable for volume of bell sound.

Snoopy won't listen in on your calls, but he rings when you get one. This fully functional SNOOPY pushbutton phone has an optional built-in desk lamp and Snoopy's head can turn a full 132 degrees in either direction to suit any mood or decor.

I'VE ALWAYS WANTED ONE OF THOSE!

Pick up the receiver, dial your number, and suddenly Snoopy spins around and around while the bell rings and rings. Plastic SNOOPY Play Phone is 9" tall.

MINI-SNOOPY

The popularity of these miniatures proves that little SNOOPY minis go a long way. SNOOPY minis measure approximately 2", are manufactured in ceramic or vinyl, and are popular all over the world. For play, decoration, or just holding in your hand, SNOOPY minis appeal to adults as well as children and are sold in retail outlets from Ohio to the Orient.

These SNOOPY Vinyl Fun Figures capture Snoopy at his best in some striking action poses.

Small wonder he can frolic and tumble. It's a SNOOPY hand-painted ceramic sculpture.

BANKS

It's fun to make deposits into a SNOOPY bank because your interest is always going up. With the many sizes and shapes to choose from, SNOOPY banks are a real bonanza. The collection includes vehicles, animals, sports themes, doghouses, eggs and rainbows! All banks have removable stoppers.

Bank styles to suit every savings account include Football, Tennis, Baseball, Hard Hat, Slicker, and Top Hat.

SNOOPY brass-plated metal bank is tarnish-resistant. 6½" high.

62

Snoopy enjoys living it up, especially if it means hitching a ride on a friendly elephant.

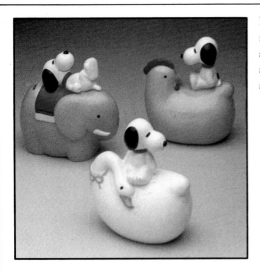

Brightly painted paper mache Animal Banks are a chicken, an elephant, and a swan. All are approximately 5" tall.

The Flying Ace readies for takeoff.

PINS

What better way to dress up the day than by wearing a SNOOPY pin? Although pins make up only part of the SNOOPY jewelry line, we present them here as a separate category because of the large number of colors, sizes, shapes, and types of pins available to choose from.

Snoopy and Woodstock, enameled of each other.

Joe Cool aims his frisbee.

Not for serious skaters
only: This SNOOPY
enameled pin measures
¾ ".

Snoopy rests on a bed of red and gold hearts.

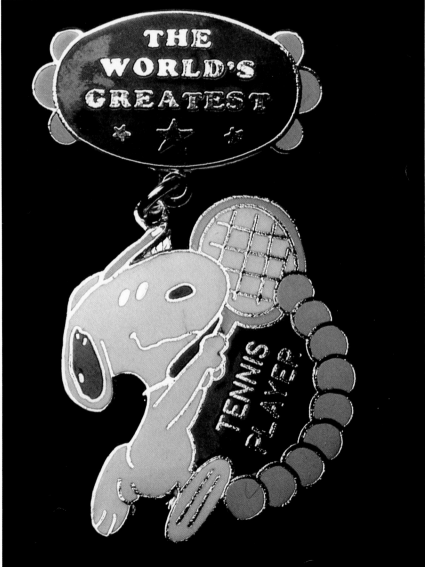

SNOOPY Award Pin balances a champ in action.

BAGS

There are so many styles and designs of SNOOPY bags that as a category they almost defy description. Almost any kind of purse, tote, or clutch bag imaginable is available, and the category also includes SNOOPY children's luggage. Most bags are made out of canvas, vinyl, or nylon, and many can be found in at least two sizes and a variety of colors.

Cotton/polyester/nylon SNOOPY Doghouse Bag is quilted inside and out and has Velcro closure. Shown here: 6"x 8" size. Also available in 4"x 6".

SNOOPY plush bag with nylon rope wrist strap has zipper back and measures 6". Larger size can be used as a pajama bag.

A SNOOPY little girl's
purse, 4½"x 6", is made
of durable canvas with a
choice of colors and
original Schulz art.

Heavy-duty canvas tote
is strong enough to carry
a bowling ball. Can be
used as a shoulder bag or
hand bag.

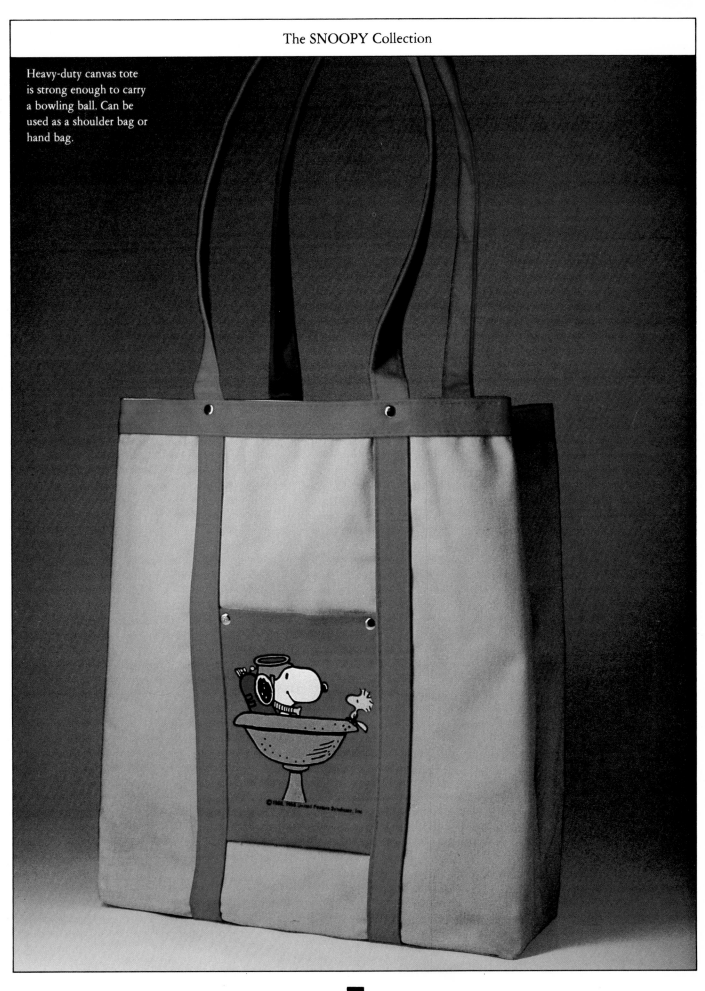

SNOOPY luggage tag has original Schulz art on the front, while your name, address, and telephone number are protected under plastic on the back.

©1958 United Feature Syndicate, Inc.

This line of SNOOPY children's luggage comes in 10'', 11'', 12'', and 13'' sizes and has key lock zipper. Nylon front and side panels clean easily with mild soap and water.

Snoopy likes to travel light and that's easy with this nylon overnight bag with adjustable nylon strap.

USEFUL KITCHEN THINGS

In the kitchen, Snoopy is more than just "man's best friend." He's also for Moms, kids, and all kinds of hosts. From cooking to cleanup, Snoopy sets a proper mood for anyone who appreciates a little extra help in the kitchen.

Nobody serves up snacks better than Snoopy in these square and circular metal beverage and snack trays.

The artful chef learns to work around the table manners of his friends. One design from the SNOOPY metal cannister series.

Everyone's room will be clean with this metal SNOOPY wastebasket to inspire neatness.

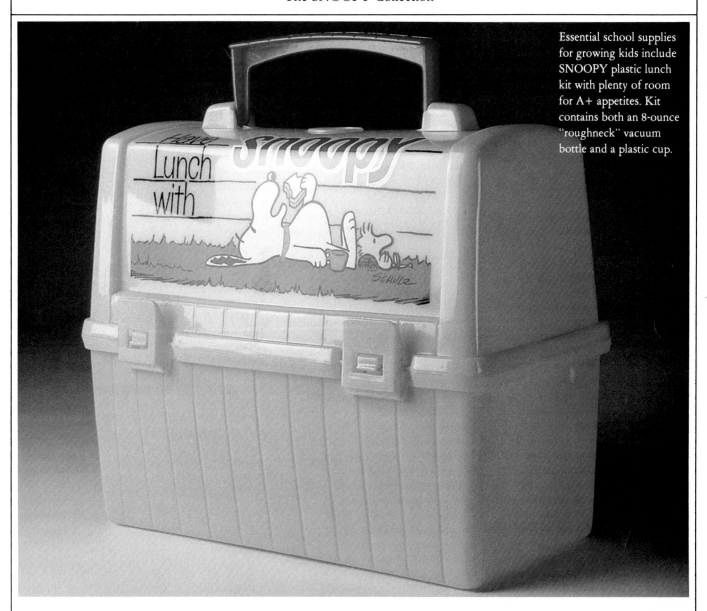

Essential school supplies for growing kids include SNOOPY plastic lunch kit with plenty of room for A+ appetites. Kit contains both an 8-ounce "roughneck" vacuum bottle and a plastic cup.

When is a dog dish a conversation piece? When Snoopy is hungry—or when it's filled with potato chips, peanuts, or popcorn for hungry human party guests. These plastic "Suppertime" dishes are available in three sizes and various colors.

MORE USEFUL THINGS

Snoopy can't stop the
rain, but looking through
his transparent vinyl
children's umbrella can
make it easier to spot the
rainbows.

Snoopy and Woodstock are always on top with this SNOOPY clock. The 17" clock has a wood box frame and is suitable for hanging anywhere.

SPORTSWEAR

The SNOOPY Sportswear Line began with T-shirts, which continue to be among the very top sellers of all the SNOOPY merchandise. Now the line has grown to cover many new fields. Jackets, sneakers, tennis and ski clothing, warm-up suits, rain gear, mittens, and swimwear represent a sampling of the SNOOPY outerwear that is currently so "in." Because the sportswear seems to appeal equally to all ages, shapes, and sizes of SNOOPY fans, it is made available in a broad range of sizes, colors, and patterns.

Right: Young women model SNOOPY long sleeve whites.
Below: Young men's sport whites and two-color shirts.

From left to right:
Placket-front baseball jersey with three-quarter length sleeves. Polyester and cotton.
Football jersey with a colored yoke shoulder that extends down the top half of the sleeves.
Top-of-the-line football jersey is knit with the "Perset" process that does away with shrinkage and fading.

CHEERS

CHRISTMAS

Each group of PEANUTS Christmas ornaments is cleverly designed, beautifully crafted and colorfully painted. These ornaments are perfect for decorating the tree, arranging on a mantel, setting on a Christmas dinner table, attaching to a package, stuffing in a stocking, or starting a collection.

It's Christmas every day in United Feature Syndicate's Licensing Division, where thousands of pieces of merchandise are on display in the big "SNOOPY Showroom." Here the perennial Christmas tree shines with a few of the scores of SNOOPY ornaments currently available.

Snoopy as Santa offers some fresh ideas for Christmas. Ceramic planter makes Christmas come alive. Actual-size ceramic SNOOPY Santa carries a little Christmas cheer in his gift bag as Woodstock watches.

This 3½" Snoopy holds a candle to Santa, while illuminating everyone's Christmas.

Silver ball tree ornaments sparkle in colorful shades of SNOOPY Christmas visions.

Six styles of 3" ceramic
full-figured Christmas
SNOOPY ornaments.

PEANUTS ceramic bells come in fifteen different patterns and three sizes from 6" to 11". Big or little, they all sound clear as a bell.

CARDS

While a large number of the SNOOPY designer paper products are scrapbooks, wall decorations, posters, wrapping paper, and party decorations, SNOOPY greeting cards started it all. The cards have been selling so well for so long time that you can send a personalized printed message from Snoopy for almost any occasion—and even non-occasions! Some of these are "Hello," "Love," "Missing You," "Retirement," "New Home," and six different types of birthday messages. As usual, the ambassador of goodwill makes staying in touch a little easier.

SNOOPY cards are "Birthday Thoughts," "Birthday Compliments," "Hello," and "Special Friend." 7"x 5".

". . .Or if I just never stopped thinking of you from yesterday." SNOOPY "thinking of you" card.

". . .O great cool one." SNOOPY birthday card.

When you fold, seal, and mail a SNOOPY Postalette, you have the warmth of a letter with the convenience of a postcard. Sets of twelve come with matching seals.

Snoopy presents an instant pick-me-up for your favorite walls: a foam-backed adhesive Wall Decoration.

CHILDREN'S CLOTHING

Come rain, snow, sleet, or fair weather, SNOOPY children's clothing will dress a child from head to toe. Durable, colorful fabrics combined with catchy SNOOPY captions and original Schulz art that gets right to the heart of what kids are all about. The message is that kids are people, too. For adults, it's just a matter of remembering how good it feels to be a child dressed up in SNOOPY clothing.

From left to right:
Alpine SNOOPY knit hat and hooded "Baseball" sweatshirt. Cotton duck baby bag and pullover sweatshirt. Watch out for adults in SNOOPY clothing.

From left to right:
Regulation SNOOPY
"Super Star" tennis hat.
Wool knit vest and ski
mittens.
Happiness is your first
SNOOPY velour warm-
up suit.

WHAT'S SNOOPY WITHOUT BELLE?

Belle, Snoopy's beautiful sister, just loves clothes. Her outfits come in two sizes to fit the small Plush Belle, 10", and the medium Plush Belle, 15". There are approximately twenty-two different styles of clothing made especially for Belle, ranging from Mrs. Santa to a Hula Girl outfit.

Stunning in her velveteen party dress, tonight Belle will trip the light fantastic.

Belle practices a sprightly "do-si-do" in her gingham square dance pinafore.

Key to Manufacturers of Products Shown

American Telecommunications, p. 57; Artex, pp. 80-81; Aviva Enterprises, pp. 64, 65, 67 (bottom), 72, 73; Aviva Toy, pp. 31, 32, 33, 34-35, 36; Butterfly Originals, pp. 68, 92, 93; Colorforms, pp. 48, 49; Determined Productions, pp. 1, 2, 4, 14, 15, 16, 17, 18, 19, 20, 21, 22, 23, 24, 25, 26, 27, 30, 37, 46, 47, 52, 53, 54, 55, 58, 60, 61, 62, 63, 69, 70, 71, 74, 75 (bottom), 76, 77, 82, 83, 86, 92, 93, 94, 95; Hallmark Cards, pp. 84, 85, 88, 89, 90-91; Hasbro, p. 56; Knickerbocker, p. 29; J.P. Stevens, pp. 44-45; King Seely Thermos, p. 75 (top); Milton Bradley Co., pp. 50-51; Oden, pp. 66, 67 (top); Osaka Nishikawa, pp. 42, 43, 78, 79; Schleich, p. 59; Schmid, pp. 38, 39, 40, 41, 87; Trimfit, p. 28.

Photo Credits

Photographs pp. 80-81 courtesy Artex, Prairie Village, KS; pp. 2, 12, 13, 16, 17, 20, 21, 23, 25, 46, 47, 52 (inset), 53 (inset), 59, 61, 63 (inset), 68, 69, 86 courtesy Determined Productions, San Francisco, CA; pp. 18-19, courtesy Familiar Ltd., Kobe, Japan; p. 10, an R. Smith Kiliper photo.